TEENS
ON THE
WITNESS STAND

Cindy Tutsch

Hart Research Center
Fallbrook, California

Edited by Ken McFarland
Cover art direction and design by Ed Guthero
Cover photo by Mark Lisk
Inside photos by Dr. Ed Norton, Richard Dower,
and John Bernet

ISBN: 1-878046-13-6

DEDICATION

To my family: My husband Ulli—faithful witnessing driver through sleet and heat; my son Karl—who has chauffeured me to many Bible study leads and taken umpteen messages from witnessing drivers; my son Mikki—official manuscript corrector and also resident chauffeur; and my daughter Liesl—who has steadfastly chosen to believe that her mommy can do anything (a source of immeasurable encouragement).

With special thanks to
Tom and Violet Zapara

CONTENTS

FOREWORD

So what's new about teen witnessing? Why write a book about it? Doesn't every academy take students out to clean up a roadside or park, sing for the elderly, or share materially with those less fortunate? And hasn't that been happening for fifty years?

The history of the computer illustrates the difference between the typical witnessing projects of the past, as compared to what God has been doing through teens in Michigan, working with the author of this book.

Computer buffs will remember the "Osborn 1." For one brief, shining moment, The Osborn 1 was the sales leader in transportable computers. It was the joy of many professional number-crunchers because it weighed under 25 pounds, had 64K of memory, and cost under $2,000.

By comparison, just six years before the introduction of the Osborn 1, we purchased a Honeywell computer system to replace the old NCR posting machine at Mid-American Health Services, where I was CEO. That Honeywell system came in a moving van and took up most of the usable space in a 16 x 20 foot room—a room that had to be climatized for both humidity and temperature. The Honeywell gobbled up 440 volts of power and boasted a whopping 16K of memory. Oh, yes—the price: $25,000, plus a hefty monthly maintenance fee and utility bill.

No wonder the Osborn was such a hot property for a few months—93 percent cheaper, 4 times more powerful, and you could even carry it around if you were physically fit and didn't have too far to go. But the Osborn soon became a museum piece. Today, the hot property is a notebook-sized computer for about the same price, but nearly 1,000 times more powerful and one-fourth the size and weight.

The changes this technological explosion has made possible are so vast that those of us not in the industry can hardly grasp their magnitude or understand their potential.

If God is to finish His work while we are alive, His church needs the kind of revolution in spiritual power symbolized by what has happened in the computer industry!

Quietly, during most of the last decade, that revolution has been in preparation on the campuses of boarding academies in Michigan, through the efforts of the author, Cindy Tutsch.

I became acquainted with Cindy's work when I accepted the presidency of the Michigan Conference. Major economic woes could have distracted academy and conference administrations from focusing on the need for the schools to be training centers for soul-winners.

An academy industry had lost $1.4 million in the first five months of its fiscal year. The conference of 20,000 members was operating five senior academies. Two were boarding schools functioning in plants utilizing less than their full capacity. Lay leadership caught the vision of what might happen if students became part of the answer to the church's evangelistic challenge. They supported the concept of an aggressive advance, while addressing the economic crisis as a secondary issue.

Elder Don Dronen, a soul-winning pastor with major strengths in personal evangelism, was moved to the Holly church to help those members work with Cindy and her students. The results were electrifying. Dr. Ed Norton joined the Michigan Conference Education Department and initiated Bible Labs in the K-10 system, in addition to helping the witnessing efforts on the academy campuses. The Lord rewarded that soul-winning thrust with surprising results.

The conference moved from five to three academies. Divested of a major losing business, it paid off a major debt caused by business losses and consolidated the two oldest boarding academies in the Adventist church. Such major trauma could have splintered the consitituency. While there were healthy debates testing the issues and information, the harmony was truly amazing.

Much of that cohesiveness can be traced to the experiences occurring in the youth witnessing and outreach activities. Parents, teachers, and committee members could all see a difference in attitudes among the students. Bible teachers reported that students were coming to class asking for help in answering questions asked by non-Adventists with whom they had been studying in the community.

The parking lot of the Cedar Lake church was full Tuesday evenings—almost as full as Sabbath—as drivers from the village came to transport students to their Bible studies. A bonding occurred between many of the drivers and the students. The generation gap was closed. And yes, there were baptisms—many of them. They included both students and adults from the community.

In the following pages, you will learn how students themselves evaluate their witnessing experience. I hope you will find new encouragement toward more direct soul-winning in your church and school. But you will get more than encouragement. This is a "how-to" book. You will discover the fulfillment of the promise on page 432 of *From Heaven With Love*: "Those who minister to others will not be longing for exciting amusements, or for some change in their lives. The great topic of interest will be how to save souls ready to perish."

And as you read, please remember the Osborn 1. Many of yesterday's computer programmers who helped get the most from the limited memory of the old mainframes have difficulty at times fully utilizing the greater flexibility of today's powerful desktop and notebook computers.

It is possible that "Youth Ministry" has for too long been viewed as a ministry *toward youth*? Why not *let youth minister*? Such a revolution could help usher in Pentecost II!

—Glenn Aufderhar,
President, Adventist Media Center

PREFACE

You say 145 teenagers from one school are currently giving Bible studies or teaching Revelation Seminars? How did it happen? What did it take to get them interested in doing this? What Bible studies are they using? How do they get to their appointments? How do they know what to say?

As the witnessing teacher at Great Lakes Adventist Academy, I often hear questions like these. I think our Outreach Ministries at GLAA are pretty miraculous myself—especially when you consider we live in the "boonies," over an hour from any large metropolitan center.

In addition, our Outreach and Witnessing class proposals initially met with quite a bit of skepticism from the doubters, the cautious, and the downright hostile-to-new-ideas bunch.

Today though, there are few skeptics, and even the hostile have become in many cases our most ardent supporters. But before we go any further into the story, I'd like to give credit where it is due:

"Not to us, O Lord, not to us, but to thy name give glory because of thy loving kindness, because of thy truth." Psalm 115:1, NASB.

Cindy Tutsch
August 1992

ACKNOWLEDGMENTS

One of the benefits of belonging to the church body is the love and support we each receive from true believers. Friends who pray together build an enduring relationship, and for those caring persons I will be grateful throughout eternity.

The events chronicled in this book have received enormous impetus through the indefatigable efforts of two outstanding leaders—Elder Glenn Aufderhar and Elder Jay Gallimore. I also appreciate Dr. Ed Norton and Dr. George Akers taking time to read the manuscript and offer helpful suggestions.

Duane Anderson, GLAA computer teacher, cheerfully offered much help throughout the whole process. And I must express my gratitude to my parents, Adolph and Jean Grams, who have daily defined for me the word *love*.

1

WELL, FOR STARTERS, JUST START!

I went to academy in the 60s. (Did they have schools and cars then? my twins sometimes ask!) Bible classes were primarily sources of information in that era, skillfully taught by dedicated men in conservative suits and ties. I learned a lot of information.

The problem was, I didn't have much use for all that "head knowledge." What do you do with memory verses, anyway, besides reproduce them on a test? Sure, knowing that "the angel of the Lord encampeth around those who fear him, and delivereth them" is great for remembering when things go bump in the night. But the biblical concept that the Good News is meant to be shared never got beyond the mere recitation of Matthew 28:19, 20.

Go out and get involved in community service? The idea never hit our academy campus, which was pretty typical of most academies at that time. So what did energetic, high-spirited, restless teens do

15

after classes in the 60s? Well, I choose not to answer that for my friends. But speaking for myself, I climbed forbidden water towers, wrote and disseminated "underground" reactionary newsletters, attended professional sporting events, listened to pop music, planned clandestine parties, spent time in the music practice room with my boyfriend, ate body- and mind-destroying foods, and occasionally wrote depressing poetry. When energy flagged, I turned to caffeine and diet pills.

None of the above strengthened my waning friendship with Jesus.

Ten years after I graduated from academy, aglow in the ardor of a renewed relationship with the patient Saviour I had neglected as a teen, I told God: "If You give me a chance at teaching Bible in academy, I promise I'll do it differently."

Something was missing from what I knew of the Bible, and as I began to study God's ideas for His schools, I came across such thoughts as this one: "The plan of the schools we shall establish in the closing years of the message is to be of an entirely different order from those we have instituted." *Counsels to Teachers*, p. 532.

Could it be that our curriculum needs revising, I wondered? What about our entertainment and recreation? Is there a relationship between what we eat and our ability to discern God's voice? And are our schools really a light in a dark place, or are we pretty wrapped up in our own interests?

As I compared the attrition rate of Latter Day Saint youth with Seventh-day Adventist youth, I observed that more LDS young people remain committed to their religion than do SDA youth— especially LDS youth who have been involved in a

"Mission"—sharing LDS religion door to door six days a week for two years. If verbally expressing one's belief in a non-biblical system or ideology strengthens one's faith in that system, I thought, how much more could be accomplished in the heart of one who is expressing the truths of Scripture?

I became convinced that verbal, go-out-in-the-highways-and-byways-and-compel-them-to-come-in style of witnessing is mandated for us all—especially for our energetic youth. They are either pawns in Satan's service or soldiers in Christ's army. Satan is *actively* recruiting—are we?

Rome wasn't built in a day, and neither is a witnessing program. Dick Tibbits had a small witnessing class at Pioneer Valley Academy, and I started by occasionally driving his students to their Bible studies. On Sundays I would pile my three pre-schoolers into the school van and take a load of teen volunteers into the community to distribute (sell or give away) Christian literature. We used the special editions of *These Times*, such as *How to Stop Smoking* and *Vegetarianism*, paperback *Bedtime Stories* and *The Bible Story*, *Bible Answers*, and *Steps to Christ*. While the students went door to door in those picturesque New England villages, I stayed in the van and read from *The Bible Story* and *Bedtime Stories* to my kiddies.

The students had some wonderful and some less-than-wonderful experiences. All the way back to academy, they'd chatter animatedly about their adventures. I was hooked.

Later, while teaching Bible at Adelphian Academy, I lobbied for my own Witnessing class. The idea met with some resistance. Apparently some believe that the only good evangelism is lifestyle modeling—that is, that after observing the purity, honesty, and devotion of a Christian, an interested person will then request baptism.

But I wonder what might never have happened had Jesus and Paul been into such passive witnessing. And think of what *has* happened when credible (loving and loveable) Christians have taken literally Christ's commission to *go* into all the world and teach! Paul even goes farther and says that salvation comes to those who *verbalize* their belief that Jesus is their Saviour and Lord (see Romans 10:10).

Another of God's messengers, writing later, also said that Christians are to *go*:

"[The disciples] were not to wait for the people to come to them; they were to go to the people with their message" (*Acts of the Apostles*, p. 28).

Eventually, though, the school leadership agreed to give active, overt evangelism a try.

"Go for it—it's all yours," I was told. And the words were meant literally. I was on my own. The first year or two, that small class of about twenty students beautified our village streets (picked up garbage!), sang in class and in rest homes, distributed Christian literature, and marked their Bibles with topical studies. We formed a seminar group and conducted the Sabbath service in many Michigan churches. But it took a seminar with Don Gray, and a new pastor, Don Dronen, to motivate me to actually have my students begin giving Bible studies in the homes of non-Seventh-day Adventists.

Our little group of students and adult drivers met on Tuesday nights at 6 p.m. in the church fellowship hall. The church deaconesses provided soup and sandwiches. Since no one had to go home or to the cafeteria for supper, we were able to squeeze in an extra half hour of instruction before the group divided into teams of three: two students and a driver.

That year the charter group witnessed several baptisms resulting from the systematic efforts of the students and adults, working under the direction of the Holy Spirit. The numbers and the blessings have been increasing ever since.

You're still not sure of every detail of how this all works? That's okay. Neither was I. Just start, and you'll find that the Holy Spirit is really the best Teacher! (See Psalm 119:99; Exodus 4:15; John 14:26; and 1 John 2:27.)

2

FINDING INTERESTS AND GIVING BIBLE STUDIES

One of the most effective ways to find Bible study prospects is through door to door surveys. Some teens actually request this approach, though for others the thought of meeting total strangers at the door elicits symptoms of sheer terror. Training teens to take a survey includes the obvious: look your contact in the eye, smile, begin your canvass with confidence, and don't pause until you've wrapped up the first question! A hesitant, unsure beginning almost invites the predictable response, "I'm sorry, I'm not interested, too busy, no thanks," et cetera. A clipboard and a pencil help the students look more credible.

Usually, I allow students to pick their own partners. I've found that two girls work fine, as does a guy and a girl, but two fellows together is sometimes intimidating to women—unless they're charming, freckle-faced freshmen! Besides, two boys surveying together are sometimes falsely identified as missionaries from another denomination. Usually the driver waits in the car as the survey is taken.

At the conclusion of the survey (see the Appendix) we leave the first two Good News lessons and a KJV or NKJV Bible paged to the lessons and tell the contact we'll be back next week to get his or her opinion of them.

If the lessons have not been completed when we return, we say, "We've set aside this time just for you. If you like, we can step inside and do the first lesson together. Sometimes it's easier to get started if you have someone with whom you can study." If the contact hesitates, we might say, "It will take us about 45 minutes to do one lesson together. If that's too long for you, perhaps we could do half a lesson."

If the contact indicates that another night would be better, we try to accommodate that desire. I encourage the students to spend quality time on the lessons themselves during the week, writing in answers, reviewing the teacher's supplements, and writing possible illustrations or important points in the margins. We purchase Good News binders for our students and write their name on the outside of the binder with black indelible ink, so that the completed lessons aren't tossed in the bottom of a locker or closet.

When the students return to the home where they left the lessons and the week's lessons have been completed, their approach goes something like this: "Hi! We came back to see how you enjoyed the lessons we left last week. Would you mind if we come in so we can go over the answers together? It will only take a few minutes."

Once the group is seated, the students take some time to visit. They might introduce themselves more thoroughly, telling their new friend where they live and perhaps a little about the school they attend and about their own family. Some students need to be cautioned not to monopolize the conversation; others will need encouragement to share a little more of themselves. The length of the study will vary—usually anywhere from thirty to sixty minutes, depending on whether the group does one or two lessons, the speed of the readers, and the duration of the preliminary visiting.

Elder Don Gray has successfully used the acronym FORT as a suggested outline of topics to discuss in this preliminary visiting. Depending on the situation, these topics might all be briefly discussed at the first visit.

F-amily. Sample questions: How long has your family lived in this area? Are these your grandchildren's pictures on the wall? How old are your children?

O-ccupation. Do you work outside your home? Do you work close by? (Sometimes preferable to the more direct "What do you do for a living?")

R-What is your religious background? (This question has been used by our students hundreds of times, and when phrased just this way, has never been offensive to the contact.)

T-estimony. This is a brief testimony of the student's own experience with God. The principles of an effective testimony can be found in the Appendix.

In subsequent visits, this preliminary visiting

should evolve naturally into a mutual sharing of some highlight from the week's activities—perhaps an answered prayer story, or a particularly happy experience. This is friendship evangelism at its best. Teenagers often find it easier to point to God as the Giver of all good gifts than do some inhibited adults!

On the other hand, a few teens, like some adults, have trouble socializing with "their people." Role playing sometimes helps, and in rare cases, where both students on the team are extremely shy or socially unskilled, I ask permission to switch partners.

After five or ten minutes of socializing, a previously appointed member of the team (at this point the team is three: two students and a driver) says something like: "It's great to visit together, but we need to get started with our lesson(s) because: (A) we'll need to get back for study hall, (B) we know you're busy, and we don't want to take too much of your time, or (C) they were so interesting this week that I'm especially eager to get started. Before we begin, let's ask God to bless our study together."

Caution: The prayer should be brief, though unhurried, asking for the Holy Spirit to help each person to understand the Word of God and *should never* include "and please help Mrs. Smith to get something out of this lesson." (Standard prayer mistake for *many, many* teen beginners!)

Remember, we are all in this together! "This" being Planet Earth. And every inhabitant of this planet has sinned and needs a Saviour. At every moment of every Bible study, we each need the Holy Spirit—learner and teacher alike.

Our format is simple and is dependent on the Spirit and the Word—not on human eloquence. One person in the group, which is now around a table or in the living room, begins by reading question one *and* his/her handwritten answer, as well as the note under the question. The next person reads question two and the accompanying note, and thus it continues around the circle. If the students have comments or illustrations or wish to stress a point, they should "jump in" with their relevant comment, even if that particular question isn't theirs.

It is important to read the commentary under the question. Repetition (Deuteronomy 6:4-7) is an essential key to learning and especially retention, and for some, the accompanying note was never read in the first place, as some persons skip over that part and only answer the questions.

The most important question in the lesson is the last one. Students need to be reminded often not to omit this thought question. In fact, they should stress it. The question might ask "Is it your desire to receive Jesus into your heart?" and it is very important that the students enlarge on the answer even if it isn't their turn to respond. For instance, at the conclusion of the lesson entitled, "Good News About the Bible," a student might say, "God's Word is becoming increasingly more important to me, and I want to take more time every day for Bible study." After the lesson on tithing, a student might say, "I've found that God is really able to stretch my money in unexpected ways after I have paid my tithe."

This testimony of the student's own experience on the topic of the study is essential! It needn't be too long—a sentence or two might be fine.

Another important component of the wrap-up is to determine how well the contact understands the lesson. Sometimes students can do an entire lesson on what happens when you die and discover that the individual still thinks that when you die, your soul floats immediately to heaven. It is absolutely essential to know where the contact is in his or her thinking on each subject before going to the next topic. Therefore, after each lesson one of the following questions should be asked:

1. Did this lesson make sense to you?
2. What is your understanding of the topic?
3. What did you see as the main point of the lesson?
4. Did you learn something new from the lesson that you didn't know before?

These four questions can be used alternately and repeated for many weeks. In fact, the first time or two, the contact may have difficulty summarizing the lesson or stating the main point. After that he or she will often study with these wrap-up questions in mind. The students themselves also need to be able to state the main point of each lesson. For many, looking for the main point takes practice and coaching.

After the final question, someone in the group should offer a concluding prayer. At this time, it is appropriate to ask God's blessing on each of the family members in the household by name. The study and the prayer should be the last thoughts left in the home. In other words, *leave immediately after the prayer.* This is not the time to chat and prolong the visit. The entire time spent in the home should not be longer than one hour, and 45 minutes is usually better. Leave them wanting more—not saturated!

Enrichment materials that may be left in the home, as the lesson might indicate, include *Steps To Christ, Open Secrets,* magazines such as *How To Stop Smoking* or *Vegetarianism,* and other donated or purchased special materials that might fit individual needs. At Christmas we gift wrap *He Taught Love* or another attractive book, and the students often write a personal message on a card.

The most important lesson in any series is the one which invites the contact to give his or her heart to Jesus, and accept Him as Saviour. We role play this lesson in class and remind the students repeatedly that this is indeed the pivotal lesson in the series. Many times my own students have made a real first-time commitment or recommitment to the Saviour as they prepared for this lesson—or during actual teaching and praying in the home.

The concluding question in the lesson on salvation should be "Is there anything that would prevent you from committing yourself to God right now?" We encourage the students to kneel with "their people" at this lesson in commitment or recommitment.

Not all Bible study contacts are found through the survey method. We also follow up ads we have placed in the newspaper, Home Health Education Service paid-out accounts, It Is Written interests, VBS attendees, *Signs* recipients, cooking school and Breathe Free attendees, and names given us by church members.

In my opinion, the best resource, by far, for detailed information on all these methods of finding a Bible study interest, and more besides, is Don Dronen's book *How Can I Find a Bible Study Interest?*, available at any Adventist Book Center.

Cindy Tutsch describing Elder Don Dronen's manual,
How Can I Find a Bible Study Interest?

Teens doing "missionary work" are disarming, there's no doubt. For this reason, teens can be very effective in working with former Seventh-day Adventists. Our approach goes something like this: "Hello! I'm Sally, and this is my partner, Angel. We're from Great Lakes Adventist Academy. We belong to a class at school that's learning what Seventh-day Adventists believe. For our project, we need to find someone in the community with whom we can do this new prophecy series on Daniel. We thought it would be easier to start with friends of the church. Would you do us a favor and study with us once a week?"

Adventists—former or current—usually appreciate reviewing the wonderful prophecies of Daniel and Revelation. Any of the series from Seminars Unlimited are good for this, but our favorites are the new Daniel series, and for those whose background or understanding is more limited, the Revelation Home Series works well.

Nowdays, we skip the soup and sandwiches on Tuesday nights and go right into a training, sharing, and prayer session at 6:30 p.m. By 7:15, all are headed out to their various destinations, and we strive to return by 8:30. (Some nights, the deans will attest, we strive in vain!) Our materials for the various lesson series are set up at the front of the church. Each team is responsible for collecting its own materials.

When the class was smaller, I drove a team out on Tuesday evenings. Today I usually organize materials in the church while I wait for the first groups to return from their study. I really like to hear the experiences "fresh off the press." Even though I'm often at the church till 9:30 or 10:00, I still can't hear all the stories. Which brings us to our next chapter: "Support Groups."

3

SUPPORT GROUPS

OK, let's approach this chapter one support group at a time. If you are in a non-boarding school situation, some of these categories may be more relevant than others.

DRIVERS: These people are definitely the backbone of the program. We use all kinds—and we love and appreciate them all. These wonderful folk donate their time, their gas,* and their love. Be sure they're insured, at least 18, squeaky clean in conversation, not inappropriately "touchy" with the opposite sex, supportive of SDA doctrine, and possess a valid driver's license.

You will need to recruit often. Consider any person in the church who passes the above criteria "fair game" and go for them. Again and again! Almost all who begin to drive for this program—even if initially skeptical—will soon come to sup-

---

*If a driver is in need, we sometimes give him or her a tank of gas from the Personal Ministries funds.

port it even if circumstances temporarily prevent their involvement. These drivers become friends with the teens, encouraging them on bad days, rejoicing with them on good days. Sometimes you might have to gently remind a driver not to dominate a study. (I'm the world's worst driver, because I can't keep quiet and let the kids do it!) Most drivers, however, keep a great balance, only participating when asked.

TEACHERS: It is important to recognize that the witnessing program is not the only worthy endeavor on campus! Our teachers at GLAA are supportive, eliminating major tests on Wednesdays and sometimes even easing the homework load on Tuesdays. Our gym teacher schedules no intramural on Tuesday nights. In return, I try to be supportive of his program, which means not scheduling student athletes for make-up Bible studies on the night they have a game.

Working together is really the key. For instance, in boarding school it's really important that the deans know where everyone is at all times—a fact that our patient deans have reminded me of several times!

ADMINISTRATORS: At a school, it's next to impossible to begin this kind of outreach without the support of your administrator. Ideally, it will be more than lip service, but don't wait for the ideal. My administrator—and I'm very grateful—does not allow intramural sports, committee meetings, class meetings, or any other conflicts on Tuesday nights. Our students do not have to choose between ice-cream feeds and Bible studies. And our administration now budgets thousands of dollars for our witnessing program.

DEANS: Our deans are super supportive. On Tuesday nights, kids from witnessing class return to the dorms anytime from 7:30 p.m. (Bible study canceled) to 10:00 p.m. (hit a deer). Not only are the deans patient with these disruptions to study hall, they routinely buoy up the depressed (Satan works extra hard on Tuesdays), listen attentively to Bible study adventures, and refuse to let kids—short of a deathbed illness—go on sick list on Tuesdays!

PARENTS: This is another vital support group. At our school, the witnessing table is a prerequisite to the class registration process. In other words, no student can sign up for any class until he or she is "recruited" for witnessing. (Contrary to popular rumor, I *do* allow freedom of choice!) Sometimes a parent will say "Mary or Johnny has to study—he/she cannot take an elective." At such times, I grind my teeth and count to ten! Parents, what about "Seek ye first the kingdom of God, and all these things shall be added unto you?" I can tell you that following the witnessing commission is like paying tithe—God blesses the other 90 percent! Some of the "other things" that may be added unto your children are a renewed spiritual commitment, poise, responsibility, public speaking ability, interest in others, knowledge of Scripture, friendships, improved devotional life, ability to converse with adults, and the skill of leading someone to Christ.

Most parents, I must add, are eager to see their children participate.

CONFERENCE PERSONNEL: Here again, for conference officials, seeing is believing. If you begin, however small, and persist, your conference will support your efforts. Our conference officers are as angels of God. They invite our group, free of charge, to our youth camp for lay ministry training sessions. They speak for witnessing class whenever asked. They support our Teen Lay Bible Ministries week-end with money and personnel. They pay most of the expenses for our Revelation Seminar. And without ceasing, they pray for us and let us know that they're praying.

PASTORS: Ideally, your pastor will not feel threatened or intimidated by your teens' witnessing efforts and will cooperate fully. I work with ideal pastors. If you don't, pray that God will change his or her heart. And don't stop praying or witnessing. (See Matthew 19:26; Proverbs 21:1; and Acts 5:25, 29.)

STUDENT LEADERS: Our class has become so large that I cannot hear every team's story of its Bible study every week. This apparent liability has become a blessing in disguise. We now have witnessing sub-groups, headed by veteran witnessing students chosen by their peers. The sub-groups have five to ten students per group and meet once a week for at least half an hour to share a devotional thought, Bible study or Revelation seminar experiences, and prayer. These sharing sessions are a real source of motivation and encouragement.

"It would be well to have an hour appointed for Bible study, and let the youth, both converted and unconverted, gather together for prayer and for the relation of their experiences. The youth should have a chance to give expression to their feelings" *Counsels on Sabbath School Work,* pp. 69, 70.

You can see that good teen witnessing is a team effort. If your team isn't quite all in place, start anyway! Put that toe in the Jordan River, and watch in awe as God parts the waters.

4

HOW ELSE CAN TEENS WITNESS?

Read that title again and grab your hat, because I'm not going to take a breath: Religious drama; conducting Sabbath school and church services; nursing home visitation; meals for seniors; Neighborhood Story Hour; Breathe Free Seminars; cooking schools; anti-substance abuse booths at malls and fairs; serving as blood drive coordinators; indoor and outdoor manual work for the elderly or physically infirm (i.e. leaf raking, storm window removal or addition, house cleaning, grocery shopping, wood chopping); church and house painting; community service work (sorting, mending, packing clothes); letters to prisoners and lonely people; cookie bakes and distribution; literature wrapping for mailing; registration for health ministries vans and booths; and banquets for civic service organizations.

Like Betty Crocker Kitchens, I can tell you that each of the above "recipes" is tried and proven by my Outreach* class, which specializes in community services. Two excellent resource tools for development of teen services are the Bible Labs Manual and Supplement, available from the Michigan Conference Department of Education, P.O. Box 19009, Lansing, MI 48901, and the NAD Christian Service Curriculum K-12.

Teens love to "make a difference." This year our class became the local solicitors for the Cystic Fibrosis Foundation. A video from the Foundation let the students know what a difference their efforts could make.

Try attending a few civic club meetings, like Lions or Kiwanis, and tell the officers how you or your kids want to help the town. Invite suggestions. Leave your name and number and check back occasionally for new ideas.

Let me tell you about four of my favorite projects:

Carson City: My conference doesn't believe teens are the leaders of "Tomorrow." Scratch out "tomorrow," substitute "today," and you have their maxim. Our executive committee believes this so much that they turned the management of an entire church—Carson City, Michigan—over to our Witnessing class! Not only do the kids preach and provide the music, they also pay the bills, clean the church, teach the Sabbath School classes (including children's divisions), and make up 98 percent of the church board!

---

*Outreach class and Witnessing class are separate at GLAA. Each is an elective and available for credit. Outreach students participate in manual community service projects, and Witnessing students give Bible studies or teach Revelation Seminars.

As their pastor, I can tell you that they are very dedicated and capable of assuming these responsibilities. Though the teens themselves have planned the format of the services, adults who attend do not feel uncomfortable. In fact, they love it! But don't take my word for this—the kids would want me to invite you to drop in sometime and see for yourself. (After all, they've already visited almost every house in town twice, and there are almost 400 houses!) We're on Highway 57 in central Michigan, right "downtown" on the north side of Main street, in the little white church painted, sign and all, by teens. If your church board is still hesitant about letting youth take up the offering, tell them about Carson City!

Matt Smith teaches a Sabbath School class at Carson City.

Felicia Cooper provides the special music.

(Above left): Ben Brower paints the highest part of the Carson City church. (Above right): Dina Morgan scrapes off old paint. (Below left): The new paint goes on. (Below right): Time out for some fun!

Revelation Seminars: We conducted a Revelation Seminar here before our current pastor, Fred Earles, arrived, but he's taught us how to raise them to a divine art! Under Elder Earles leadership, our Revelation Seminars have expanded into a beautiful experience for many teens. The students teach the lessons in small groups of five to eight at a table. The groups go over the questions and answers in each lesson, and then all return to the chairs set up in the center.

At this point, the presiding pastor or lay person summarizes the lesson in about a ten-minute capsule, then gives the quiz. After that, we show a video that correlates with the day's lessons. This whole process only takes about an hour and a half and is tremendously effective.

It really helps to have the support of the local church members, whose attendance helps keep morale strong, even if some non-SDAs drop out. We usually hold these Revelation Seminars in the church, but occasionally rent a hall.

Juan Smith gives a Revelation Seminar lecture.

(Above): Richard Barnum (right) was baptized after a Revelation Seminar taught by student Steve Slikkers (center). Elder Fred Earles (left) placed special emphasis on training students to give the Seminars. (Below): Brad Hall teaches a Revelation Seminar lesson.

Children's lessons: If you or your teens are still nervous about studying the Bible with an adult, consider studying with children. Marge Gray has put together a wonderful book called *Good News for Today Kids' Lessons*. Little ones love having teenagers study with them—especially if they bring stickers and occasional prizes. Prizes might include pencils with Bible verses, Bible coloring books, and such novelty items as are found inexpensively at a religious book store. One way to find children to study with is to visit those who attended Vacation Bible School. Check with the parents first to make sure they don't mind, and then explain the format to the children, showing them how the Bibles we give them are paged to the lesson books to make it easier to find the answers. All of the children with whom we are now studying love their teen mentors and look forward to Tuesday nights. In several cases, we have begun studies with the parents of the children with whom we were initially studying.

Student Tamara Ras teaches a children's lesson to Genevieve Brechting.

Detroit Youth Challenge: In the summer of 1991 I had the exhilarating experience of being the coordinator for an ASI project for teens. Thirty teenagers converged on the city of Detroit to do ten weeks of evangelism. Our program had four components: book sales, Revelation Seminars, community service work, and Sabbath services conducted at area camp meetings and churches. The students were paid 100 percent of their book sale proceeds, because the Michigan Conference donated the *He*

The Detroit Youth Challenge Team.

Taught Love books—a special edition of *Christ's Object Lessons*. They were also given a $1,000 scholarship if they satisfactorily completed the ten-week program. To qualify for the scholarship, each student was required to sell books 20 hours per week, help teach a Revelation Seminar two evenings per week, attend the Friday night Youth Challenge vespers, help conduct a Sabbath service each week, and participate every Sunday in three hours of group community service work. This work included assisting at a soup kitchen, beautifying a municipal park, helping build a local SDA church, and distributing literature and enrollment cards for Bible lessons.

Five SDA colleges and two academies gave a tuition bonus of 25 percent of whatever monies the student earned through the Detroit Youth Challenge.

The students were able to defray their tuition expenses considerably through this program, but the spiritual rewards were even greater. Here are some of their comments:

"When I first heard about the Detroit Youth Challenge, I thought I could handle what we were supposed to do. But when the first day out canvassing came, I learned I was really mistaken. People weren't always as kind and nice as I thought they would be. I learned right away that prayer is a major factor in making it through the day!

"I learned that I must trust in God, and He will always help me to find the right people some time in the day. The experiences I have had will stick with me everywhere I go and will last the rest of my life."—*Carli Sullivan*

"This Youth Challenge program has meant a lot to me, because if it hadn't come to Detroit, I don't know what I would have done during the summer. It has really enhanced my growing with God. It has also taught me how to work diligently without quitting. I really thank God for the memories that I've made this summer."
—*Jelani Grady*

Jelani Grady gives his canvass for
He Taught Love *at the door.*

"Being part of the Detroit Youth Challenge is one of the best things I ever did in my life. If I hadn't decided to participate this summer, I would have missed out on something grand and special. I feared this might have been one boring program, but it wasn't. I had so many good experiences this summer that I can't count all of them. I met a lot of people who needed someone to talk to them. They also needed someone to tell them about Jesus. I need to talk to people about Him too, so my own faith would grow.

"One day I was working in a Detroit suburb called Livonia. It was a pretty hard day. I didn't get that many books out. After supper I was walking down a dirt road. I was at one of my last houses of the day. I knocked on the door and a lady answered the door and said, 'I am on the phone right now, and I can't buy anything.'

"I started to walk away and she said, 'Wait a

minute, what do you have there?' I turned back and showed her the book. I didn't even have to say a word. She looked at the picture of Jesus on the front and went wild. She hung up the phone, pulled me inside the house and ran into just about every room in her house to hunt for money. She ended up giving me ten dollars—in change!

"Now I feel it doesn't matter what happens to you during the day, just as long as you help one person turn toward Jesus."—*Victor Roach*

"This summer was one of the most difficult summers of my life. I was very hesitant about working with the program because I said that I would never be a literature evangelist. But since I am writing this, I obviously changed my mind!

"Working in the program taught me a lot of things, such as how to handle rejection, how to be able to read a person quickly, and how to be able to share my faith in subtle ways but still let the people know what I believe.

"One of the neatest experiences I had was when I was working in Davison. It was an extremely hot day and the donations did not seem to be coming easily, though I had tried just about every way possible to get the people to take the book. I was working on one side of the street, while my partner, Melissa, worked the other.

"I went up to a door, knocked, and discovered I was knocking on the garage door! The lady came to a window and asked what I wanted. I gave her my canvass and was almost sure that she wasn't going to take the book. When I showed her the book, she had disapproval written all over her face. She did allow me to finish the canvass, but then she said that she was from a different religion and she had her own beliefs. She asked me to leave. I told her 'OK' with a smile, and I turned and left.

"I finished off a little court and saw Melissa stopped by a car. I finished my canvass, and Melissa came up and told me that the lady who had asked me to leave had driven up to her, asked if she was working with me, and had written me a check for fifteen dollars. She said, 'I just can't reject the Lord.' This experience was one of many that showed me how the Holy Spirit works on people even after we leave the door."
—*Brad Hall*

"In all my thirteen years of life, I have never prayed and asked for God's help so much as this summer! Being part of the Detroit Youth Challenge experience taught me that prayer is the key to success in canvassing.

"It was a Tuesday—my first eight-hour day— and it was 90 degrees. Sweat was literally pouring down my face. By 5 p.m. I had to admit I hadn't done very well, even though I had stopped before each row of houses to pray.

"When I decided to pray before each house, things started to pick up fast! At the first home where I had asked God to make the people receptive to the book, the guy took the book and gave me a crisp, ten-dollar bill. I said 'Wow! Prayer really works!' I prayed for the people in the next house. Then I found the guy out watering his lawn. Before I even finished my canvass, the guy from the previous house was shouting, 'I gave the kid ten dollars!' So the lawn waterer also gave me ten dollars. I prayed for the work at the next house while I was walking, and the lady there didn't let me finish my canvass before she said, 'I already know what you're doing from listening to my neighbors. Here's ten dollars!' Now that's what I call positive peer pressure!

Chris Hashikawa

"From there on I have prayed at every single door without exception. It's not the money that motivated me to pray. It was the Spirit of God moving these people's hearts that drove me to pray. I know I will always remember the experience I had this summer, and with God's help heed His command: 'Rejoice evermore, pray without ceasing. In everything give thanks, for this is the will of God in Christ concerning you'" 1 Thessalonians 5:16-18.—*Chris Hashikawa*

"This summer God taught me what the saying 'You can't judge a book by its cover' really means. Judging things by appearance was a constant habit of mine. However, an experience in Detroit Youth Challenge helped change that.

"It was toward the afternoon, in the heat of the day. I was dragging my feet down a long, winding road, discouraged because I had done poorly all day. The fact that the houses were far apart didn't help much. My heart sank as I came across a dilapidated house. The lawn looked like it hadn't been cut in several months and was cluttered with car parts, et cetera. We are supposed to go to every house, but I was tempted to accidentally skip this one! However, something impressed me to go and knock on the door.

"A woman came to the door with a huge frown and hair that looked like she had just gotten off of a roller coaster. This situation really didn't look good, so I prayed extra hard and said my canvass. When I said this book was about Jesus, she smiled, and to my surprise brought a twenty-dollar bill for the book.

"I thought of the text 'For the Lord sees not as man seeth; man look on the outward appearance, but God looks on the heart.' 1 Samuel 16:7. Through the Detroit Youth Challenge experiences, I have been given more courage by God to do things that don't look appealing, such as speak in front of churches. Now I feel I have become better fit to do God's work."—*Andrew Hashikawa*

"This summer has been a very busy and rewarding one. Instead of working at a fast-food place or even not working at all, I have met many different people, some of whom are rude—but at least everyone that I have met has been willing to listen to what I had to say.

"I remember one day I was hot and thirsty and a little discouraged. I walked up to a house and rang the bell. A lady came to the door, crying. I introduced myself and told her what I was doing. As soon as she saw the book, she wanted it and stopped crying to look through it. I told her it was about the parables of Christ. As soon as I said that, she got real excited and asked if it was about Jesus. When I said 'yes,' she went back into the house and brought me a donation for the book.

"I was glad I was there to make her feel a little better as I spoke about Jesus. After that, I didn't feel as hot or thirsty anymore. That one experience encouraged me for the rest of the day. I thank God that I am able to do this work this summer."—*David Hubbell*

"This summer I learned many things, not necessarily just about selling books! For example, sugar. People always told me that if you eat it, it brings you up but then puts you way down. I didn't believe that until the first day I canvassed. I had a milkshake on an empty stomach. Within a few hours, I was so tired I could barely stand up straight. After a couple of days I realized (with Mrs. Tutsch's help) that I would have more energy without those milkshakes!

"As far as experiences go, I am a man of many stories. Some bad, some good, some embarrassing, some tremendous. Overall, my experiences have given me a great view of what people are like. The most memorable experience was when I was so tired—because it was hot and humid—that as I was walking up the stairs to a porch, I tripped and fell. The book flew from my hands to the feet of the lady who had just opened the door. She laughed, and I gave my canvass while lying prone on her porch. She helped me up, invited me in for some water, and bought the book. That helped me realize that no matter how hopeless the situation may seem, God always has a plan."—*Michael Nolden*

"It was Friday. I was having a terrible week selling. I was very depressed for personal reasons, which had something to do with my melancholy personality. I went to knock on this one door, and to my surprise there were five bikers inside. One biker said 'Hey, man, don't you get it? We're not interested!' Then two of the bikers answered back in unison 'Don't bug us around.' I asked, 'Are you interested in this book?' and they answered back, 'No, does it look like it?' Then the fourth biker said 'Hey, man, take some advice, son. Get lost before a fight breaks out.'

"I was about to leave, and the last biker said, 'I'll take it' and said to his buddies, 'You see, boys, Jesus was cool. He wasn't no stupid yuppie scum.' I gave him the book and left.

"This summer has given me memories I will never forget and experiences that will help me in whatever field that I go into."—*Jim McKinley*

"The summer of the Detroit Youth Challenge is one I will never forget. I've learned many things about our God and all the wonderful ways in which He works. Through this program I learned that I cannot depend on myself alone, especially in the area of finishing God's work. I must surrender myself to Jesus and let Him work through me. I could not have reached people door to door without the power of Jesus.

"This summer I also learned how awesome prayer is. I saw how God answers the large and small prayers. If a day got discouraging and people seemed uncaring, I would stop and pray, and then God would do something—sometimes even small—to get my spirits up so that I could continue the work of spreading the gospel. Anything taken to God in prayer, He hears. I have learned to trust God with everything.

"This summer I have seen people who really

need the Lord. I met people who had never even heard of Jesus—people who had been searching and people who refuse to admit that they need Jesus. I feel that God has used the students of the Detroit Youth Challenge to reach all these different people to plant a seed for Him!

"Not only have I been able to work for Jesus and share His love, but also my relationship and commitment to Him have increased throughout this summer. I would encourage anyone to enter this program if given the chance."—*Maggie Hill*

"One of the biggest temptations in the canvassing work is to become a shrewd gambler, only going to the homes where the odds of a sale seem in your favor. Although I usually go to every house, this summer I had started skipping houses where construction workers were the only ones present, because usually they'll say, 'I can't talk—I'm on company time.'

"I had just skipped such a house on my last street for the day when I suddenly felt a strong need to go back. As I walked in, I heard someone working upstairs, so I shouted 'Hello!' Hard rock was blaring so loud from the radio downstairs we couldn't hear each other, so I switched it off. This startled the worker, because immediately he appeared at the stair railing and asked what I was doing! Because the stairs were still under construction, I didn't want to go up them, so I said 'Here, catch.' He caught the *He Taught Love* book, and I gave him the canvass.

"He replied that he wasn't into the 'Christian stuff,' but that he would like to read the book for historical purposes. I thought to myself, regardless of why you read the book, it will still transform your life, for 'it is the power of God unto salvation' Romans 1:16.

"Now I know that the Holy Spirit sent me there. This summer I have found that by spending earnest time in study and prayer with Him each morning, I can receive the same 'power of God unto salvation.'"—*Tom Gammon*

"Monday is always a hard day to start, and this Monday was no exception. We were working apartments, which tend to be unusually difficult. Finally someone opened the door, and I was given the opportunity to present my canvass. But before I got through, the man stopped me by raising his hand. He pointed to his mouth and to his ears, and I realized he was deaf and mute. Totally confused as to what to do at this point, I simply handed the book to him. When he saw the picture of Christ on the front, not a word he could have said would have expressed his appreciation more than the look on his face. He placed the book on the table and left the room. He returned with a sizeable donation. When I left, he signed, 'Jesus loves you' in sign language.

"Through experiences such as this throughout the whole summer, I know that through Christ there is one language of love. I chose this occupation for the summer because it presented me with an opportunity to make enough money to return to academy. But I never realized how much the Lord would really bless my choice both in finances and experience.

"As the summer progressed, I came to the understanding that to present Christ at the door of each house, He has to live in my heart first. For this reason my personal devotions became the highest priority of the day. From them I could leave the house feeling confident that the Lord was with me. His protecting hand was felt many times. He also gave me the courage to go to the next door. Though some doors were slammed in my face, Christ walked with me at each door, and I know He will continue to walk with me through life."—*Robin Hansen*

"This summer I learned how the Holy Spirit works on the hearts of the people we are canvassing. One particular ten-hour day, we had been working in an upper middle class subdivision. I had been having a very good day financially, but I kept getting donations without getting a book into the home. As I was going up to a particular house, I prayed extra hard for the Holy Spirit to work on these people's hearts so I could get a book into the home. The lady that came to the door was very rude, told me she wasn't interested in hearing about my project, and slammed the door.

"I started walking down the driveway. I was very disappointed that I had not been able to get a book into the home. But as I walked down the driveway, the lady came back out of the house and asked me if I was selling something. I told her quickly about what we were doing. She seemed really interested in the book, took it, and gave me a good-sized donation besides! It's amazing how God works on people's hearts. I pray that the Holy Spirit will continue to work on her heart and that she will read the book.

"The Holy Spirit was able to work on my own heart this summer. Through this job I have

grown a lot closer to God, and I have learned to depend on Him as a personal Friend. Projects like this are what keep me active in the church."
—*Shirley Dovich*

Shirley Dovich gives her testimony on Witnessing Sabbath. (See also pages 85-88 in the Epilogue.)

"When I first began this program, I was very hesitant. I was not sure if I was outgoing enough and persuasive enough to go door to door. The first few houses I came to, either no one was home, or no one came to answer the door. Thoughts ran through my mind like 'If this is what this summer is going to be like, I'm going home!' But that first day God gave me an experience I'll never forget.

"I went to a house and knocked on the door. No one came, so I knocked again. A lady walked over from behind the house, and I explained to her what I was doing. She looked at the *He Taught Love* book and asked me a lot of questions about it. After talking for awhile, I started to become at ease and more talkative, and my voice almost stopped shaking. The woman invited me in and wrote me out a check. Then she told me that she felt I was God-sent. She had been looking for a devotional book but had not found one she liked. She told me that she probably would not have ever gotten one and that she was looking forward to reading the book.

"Then I left. As I walked down the street, my outlook had totally changed. I was now focusing on how God could impress the hearts of the people that I came in contact with, and how God would give me the power to do the work that He had called me to do!

"I'm so thankful the Detroit ASI chapter made it possible for us students to help Detroit by spreading God's love. By sharing the love I have for Christ with others, my relationship with Him has grown. I'm so glad for all the miracles I have seen God work this summer."—*Marlene Leaman*

"I went to a door and rang the bell. A man came and said he wasn't interested, before I ever said one word. When I heard him, he sounded like he was tired of people coming to the door, so I just turned around to leave. He said 'Wait a minute, I haven't even heard what you're doing!' He said he would take the book, and he gave me a good donation for it. This is just one of many experiences that happened to me this summer that show how the Lord will impress people's hearts when the human outlook is discouraging.

"I'm glad I had the opportunity to be in this program, because it has helped me to learn to trust one hundred percent in the Lord at all times. The one thing I am waiting for is to go to heaven and meet some of the people that met

Jesus through the books I left in their homes."
—*Stephen Deark*

Several of the students were from the Detroit area and were able to stay at home, and the rest were housed free of charge by church members in greater Detroit. These members provided breakfast for their teen workers. The teens either ate out or packed a lunch for the other meals. Several students had cars, and I had the school van, so we were able to divide into five sub-groups. The Home Health Education Service provided able training and leadership periodically through the summer.

If you're considering a program of this nature, I can attest to the magnitude of both the work involved and the benefits derived.

The following were essential to the success of our summer Youth Challenge programs:

1. Prayer—corporate and individual. The more, the better, I can guarantee.

2. Cooperation of ASI, conference officials, parents, pastors, church families, schools, and HHES.

For a detailed summer literature manual for organizing your group, write to the Rocky Mountain Conference. The Rocky Mountain Conference is also piloting both a 6-month or 12-month literature program for 18-25 year olds who are uncertain of their career choice or who do not have the money to go or return to college. This well-organized, highly motivational, and spiritual program will provide young adults with Christian friends, adventure, experience in meeting people, and money besides! The youth will work in groups, following much of the structure of the summer program described above.

General
Conference
President Elder
Robert Folken-
berg joins DYC
teens at the
national ASI
Convention.

National ASI
President Ray
Hamblin
encourages
teens at a DYC
vespers.

Literature
evangelist Larry
Hubble helps
orient a DYC
team.

Prayer was an essential for success before canvassing began each day.

A final check of the map before heading out.

The sun is shining! Let's go!

Jason Lim gives a canvass!

Team members canvassed people wherever they could find them.

DYC teens shared their experiences at a different church each Sabbath.

Cindy Tutsch listens to the week's adventures at a DYC vespers.

Friday night DYC vespers always ended with singing "Side By Side We Stand."

Everyone loved the potlucks after a DYC church service!

5

THE KIDS AND I PHILOSOPHIZE

I teach senior Bible. One of the requirements for this class is to do a specified amount of volunteer community service work every quarter. This type of requirement is becoming more and more common in public schools.

"Volunteerism," a "thousand points of light," "community citizen"—under various headings, the message is the same—do something charitable for someone besides yourself. The Old Testament prophets tell us repeatedly to care for the poor, release the bonds of the oppressed, and show mercy to the less fortunate. Jesus not only preached the same message, He exemplified the call to service by His own lifestyle. And Ellen White says:

"True education is missionary training. Every son and daughter of God is called to be a missionary; we are called to the service of God and our fellow men, and to fit us for this service should be the object for education" *The Ministry of Healing*, p. 395.

So I require service for my senior Bible classes, and admittedly, some seniors initially enroll in witnessing class more out of a desire to meet the service requirement than from unadulterated altruism. By the end of the year, however, there are few who haven't experienced major motivational change.

Here's how the teens describe their experiences and feelings about witnessing:

Tell something about your Bible study or Revelation Seminar.

We are getting to be close friends. My hopes are that these people will really make Jesus their true friend. M.Y.

My Revelation Seminar people are great! They are interested in learning and ask challenging questions. I hope to see them all baptized soon. M.S.

I'm studying with children. Even if they aren't able to continue coming to church, I hope that when they grow up and are looking for something in their life, they well remember the studies they took as children. K.S.

How is giving Bible studies different from what you expected?

I never realized how little some people know about God. I grew up as a Seventh-day Adventist, and I've always known stories like Daniel in the lions' den and David and Goliath. But there are people who have never heard these stories that are as common to me as Jack and the Beanstalk to them. W.K.

I expected to be teaching these people all these wonderful things I had learned since childhood, and it ended up them teaching me! M.H.

I expected it to be very intimidating going into someone's home and teaching, when I myself am still learning. But when I actually got to meet my Bible study person and got to know him, it was very easy to go over the lessons and learn from them. S.S.

I didn't think I would really take the Bible studies seriously. Many times I felt like dropping witnessing class, but I didn't. I really grew attached to my Bible study person, and am proud of her living for the Lord. R.O.

My Bible studies were a lot easier than what I had expected. I have had great and friendly Bible studies. I wouldn't hesitate to give another one at all. It has been fun. R.J.

I was afraid I wouldn't be able to answer all the questions, but I found I knew more than I thought I did. T.P.

I didn't really expect my relationship with my study to be as great as it is. Sharon is a close friend of mine, and I wouldn't want it any other way. E.S.

I wasn't really sure what to expect. I knew that I was very scared and unsure of myself. But with prayer and study, I was able to overcome being scared and do my best to explain the lessons. J.S.

I thought it would be hard and that I wouldn't

be able to answer her questions. Actually, it is a lot easier than I thought it would be, because she is attentive and isn't afraid to ask questions when she doesn't understand. C.Z.

A lot easier—giving the studies is just half of it—the friendship is great! R.S.

It is really not as hard as I expected. God gives me words to speak. E.M.

I was surprised to find myself in it head first, leading out in the study. A.M.

Really all it is, is sharing what I know about the Bible with someone else, singing with them, and praying together. I can't even count how many different teenagers from around the neighborhood have joined us for the study at this house. C.K.

It is more fun than what I heard. J.L.

I expected to know absolutely nothing about what I was teaching, but after studying the lessons I realized that I did know! M.J.

I didn't think I knew enough about the Bible to do a very good job. But these lessons were easy to work with, and if a question came up that I didn't have the answer for, I just told them I'd find the answer next week and bring it for them to study. T.K.

My study is so different from the others that I truly feel God knew what I could answer and gave me the right study. I'm having a lot of fun and wouldn't change the experience for anything. L.L.

How has your life changed since you started giving Bible studies or teaching Revelation Seminars?

It has made me more aware of my beliefs. And less ashamed of expressing them. M.H.

It has made me feel like I can change. I have failed so many times that sometimes I don't feel that I can get back up off my face, but hearing the spiritual experiences of my fellow students and the people I study with has given me the encouragement that I need to keep on my upward climb to be with our Lord. M.N.

I've had to study the Bible a lot more, and the more I read, the closer I get to God. N.C.

I've become more interested in being involved in church things, and I actually don't mind going to church! R.O.

Giving Bible studies has helped me establish proof for what I believe, and it's helped me to be able to share more openly. S.S.

I have realized that God really can work through one person, to help make an impact on someone else's life. J.S.

As I give studies, I also learn from the lessons. E.D.

It's shown me that witnessing to others isn't as hard or embarrassing as I thought. C.Z.

Because of this class, I was rebaptized and rededicated my life to Christ. M.L.

When I did the study on baptism, I realized

this was a step I needed to make myself. I was baptized last May. A.S.

I find that I trust God more because I can see Him work with both me and my Bible study. S.S.

It has given me more confidence in talking to others about Jesus. J.L.

Doing the lessons has given me a place to begin in my own Bible study. I have felt the need in my life for daily devotions, and this keeps me motivated to have them. L.H.

I never read my Bible or had devotions until this year. I always prayed, but not like I find myself praying now. We always tell her [my Bible study interest] to have faith, and it made me think, "I've got to have faith, too." I never thought of that before. M.J.

I see how important it is to stand up for my standards as a Christian. My beliefs have become more valuable to me. M.M.

It has really helped me choose more and more each day to follow Jesus and let Him lead in my life. I've been struggling, but knowing that I'm a witness to others helps me grow stronger with God. L.L.

I have started studying the Bible more in depth. It has become more important to me to know exactly what I believe and why. The Bible has really come alive for me. T.C.

My closeness to the Lord has grown in many ways these past few months of school. At first I was unsure about the whole deal. Now I'm happy to say I've given my heart to the Lord and will be baptized May 11. G.B.

I've found out more about God and decided to get baptized myself. G.H.

Since I started giving Bible studies my freshman year, I've felt closer to God and studied more than I have ever before on my own. P.K.

My Bible studies have made me take a closer look at how strong my faith really is and at how much I actually know about my religion. T.P.

It has given me courage to teach about Jesus to others. A.B.

Giving Bible studies to someone is something I never dreamed about doing. I am learning about God along with giving the Bible study. It has brought me closer to Him. E.S.

I know now that studying the Bible is not always boring. J.M.

What is one of your favorite things about the study?

My favorite thing was when Sandy said she wanted to be baptized! N.C.

My study said she's interested in being baptized. E.M.

One of my favorite things about witnessing is the talks with my driver after the study. When I'm down, she cares and listens, and when things are going right, she is happy with me and shares my enthusiasm. R.H.

One time the family ran out of food, and their

sewer system leaked into the water system. We left and got all the food and water we could find and brought it to them. There were tears in Shirley's eyes. M.J.

I like the times when we share personal ideas and thoughts. I also will always cherish the friendships that were created because of those studies. I'll never forget the time when one of the people I was studying with was asked what he was thankful for, and he said that he was thankful for his Bible study. T.K.

One of my favorite things about our study was our Christmas party that we planned for them. We decorated cookies, played Christmas music, sang, read stories and had a gift exchange with gifts we had to make by hand. It was a lot of fun, and it helped us get to know each other better. K.C.

I didn't know that they were so friendly. It was easy to break the ice. We could converse about our lives and the lesson without feeling like it was a teacher/student relationship. It was like one friend teaching another friend about Jesus. R.J.

I can't remember a particular study that stands out, because they are all really special in their own way. P.K.

I enjoy the fact that Mrs. Blank enjoys our study. She looks forward to the time when we come to the door. She reads E.G. White books almost continuously. She also enjoys visiting with us. Her enthusiasm is infectious, and my partner and I never come away from a Bible study without being refreshed and rejuvenated. T.C.

My Bible study told us that she had prayed, the day before we asked her if she would take the studies, that God would send a way for her to get to know Him again, and she believed we were her answer to prayer. T.E.

I like to see the excitement in her face when she learns something new. It makes me remember when I first learned the things she is learning now. J.M.

Why would you encourage others to get involved?

It's not as "preachy" as you think it is, and you'll be really glad you took that time to make friendships and become closer to God. W.B.

You meet interesting people. Plus find out maybe you didn't know much about what our church teaches. Plus, it's a change of pace once a week. M.N.

No matter what, taking the class will help you in some way. R.O.

I was always interested in giving studies in my home church. I tried to develop some Bible studies, but it never worked out. So when I heard about the witnessing program, I decided to join. I enjoy it more than I thought I would. It has been a great experience. B.S.

My ladies seem to be eager to come to the Revelation Seminars each week. They told me that they look forward to coming and that I'm their teacher, and that makes me feel pretty special. J.S.

You will gain self-esteem through the knowledge that you're doing something good. P.G.

Because we have a very important message to spread to the world, the time and pleasure invested in this will reward us far more than a life of "sitting on our duffs." R.S.

You feel good making other people feel good. A.M.

Because people need to know what we have to share, no matter how little we think we have to give. A.S.

You learn to have patience and tact, and it's a break from the routine. R.H.

Because it is great fun, and it makes Jesus and spiritual things more real! M.M.

It is very rewarding. Anyone can do it with God's help. T.K.

It is a very good feeling to see someone draw closer to God and know I had a part of it. It also helps me draw closer to God and makes me feel better about myself. P.K.

Because I've always been told "It is more blessed to give than to receive"—and a Bible study is no different. I probably receive a greater blessing than my Bible students. S.S.

And how does the experience affect students' lives after they've graduated?

"Whenever I share my testimony of how I

came to know Jesus as my personal Friend and Saviour, it always begins with my classes taught by Aunt Cindy (as affectionately called) at Adelphian Academy. That was eight years ago. To this day, I can remember the strong impressions of the Holy Spirit that I had never experienced before, about the very soon coming of Jesus. It placed in my heart a longing desire to help others to know about this imminent surprise to most of the world.

Kelly Palmeter

"These impressions deepened as we studied verse by verse through Revelation in witnessing class and read *Final Wars* (GC), *Project Sunlight*, and *Pilgrim's Progress* in Bible class. The call to personal evangelism has not left me through the years.

"My introduction to the Spirit of Prophecy in that class opened a whole treasure house to me. I read others of her [Mrs. White's] books—*The Desire of Ages* and *Messages to Young People*. I wanted so much to share with others this precious joy that I had never known before. The opportunity came to colporteur during my summers in college, and thus many others were able to have these treasures in their home.

"The last two years the door opened to work with the Restore Project in Seattle—a conference-sponsored city evangelistic effort. It is the greatest and most satisfying joy to see people's lives turn around as they come to know Jesus.

"Now I'm finishing my formal education in a religion major, with the dream of being able to also teach a witnessing class that will help many young people to experience the joy of laboring in this harvesting season."—*Kelly Palmeter*

"The witnessing class I took in academy has monumentally influenced my life. First, it invigorated my devotional life by providing many new insights to study and experiences over which to pray. It prepared me to give an answer to anyone about my faith and beliefs.

"The class also changed the way I relate to people. Through selling literature and giving personal testimonies and classroom Bible studies to non-SDAs, I lost my fear of speaking about Christ. This has prompted me to seek opportunities in every place I have been, to witness for Jesus.

"The impact of that class has been so precious I tremble to think where I would be if I had not taken it. It has affected my choices of friends, education, activities, and jobs, while helping me be an active church member wherever I go. Praise God for making us partners in others' salvation."—*Esther Baker*

"I felt that witnessing is an essential part of the Christian lifestyle. It *is* the Christian lifestyle. I found out how true this really is when I worked in the Detroit Youth Challenge. My spiritual life had never held so much meaning, and my relationship with God had never been so vital to me, as when I was out every day witnessing.

"Now that I'm at Andrews University, I've found it harder to become involved in structured witnessing activities, so it's been a main focus of mine to find witnessing opportunities for myself. I've started a Bible study group in my dormitory, which keeps on growing in size each time we meet. I've also been involved with two of my friends in proposing that a minor in mission service be offered here at Andrews University. It's very exciting to see how students *can* take the initiative to open up all sorts of different mission opportunities.

"I've also seen that one part of witnessing is just living the Christian life. I received a call from a fellow student (whom I'd never met before) who had seen me at Wednesday night prayer meeting and wanted to know if I'd like to start a study group next quarter. This was especially exciting, because he's just now becoming interested in Christianity, and he wants to learn more about God.

"I don't think that students should be afraid to take the initiative, whatever their goal may be. I think one effective witness comes from the life you lead, and I feel that it's important for students to be willing to live out their Christianity."—*Charissa Craw*

Keep on reading now, though some of you will cry that I've quit preaching and started meddling! You may not agree with what I'm about to say next, but before you burn this book, please pray about these ideas.

I believe that the highest of all sciences is the science of "soul saving" and that an Adventist school whose students are not actively, overtly engaged in soul winning has lost its mission. Furthermore, I believe that every student—Adventist or non-Adventist—who attends our schools should be able to state clearly and concisely what Seventh-day Adventists believe in every major doctrine and back that statement with scripture.

After all, Peter says, "Be ready always to give an answer to every man who asks you a reason for the hope that is in you."

Ellen White says in *The Great Controversy*, p. 605: "None but those who have fortified their minds with the truths of scripture shall stand through the last great conflict." Can we put that another way and say that if our minds are *not* fortified with scripture, we will *not* stand through the last great conflict?

Here's another thought-provoking statement:

> "It does not seem possible to us now that any should have to stand alone; but if God has ever spoken by me, the time will come when we shall be brought before councils and before thousands for His name's sake, and each one will have to give the reason of his faith. Then will come the severest criticism upon every position that has been taken for the truth. We need, then, to study the word of God, that we may know why we believe the doctrines we advocate"—Ellen G. White, *Review and Herald Articles*, Dec. 11, 1888, p. 786.

It concerns me that many young people graduate from our schools with barely a foggy notion as to why we believe as we do. A while back I was teaching an adult Sabbath School class of about forty members. Some of the members were "pillars," you know, deacons and elders—the spiritual leaders of our church. I asked them to shut their Bibles for a moment and tell me, even loosely paraphrased, three places in Scriptures where we find out what happens when we die. None but the pastor were able. So I asked for just two texts. Still only the pastor could respond. Would you believe, not one other person could come up with even one text, without opening a Bible, to support the Adventist position of what happens when you die?

Many of these people had attended our schools. My opinion is that they undoubtedly learned those texts sometime. But if the references aren't used in sharing the good news, they go the way of much factual learning that is mastered only for a test. If we don't begin using these texts in actual Bible studies while we're young, most of us won't pick up the practice as the years advance.

Right now, we've got several children from Junior and Earliteen Sabbath School going out with our academy youth—and loving it! That Junior leader is right on target. And she is not stopping with Bible studies, but already has her kids involved in a variety of community service projects. My hunch is that those children are learning a lifestyle that most of them won't abandon.

Most of us can recite these familiar words: "With such an army of workers as our youth, rightly trained, might furnish, how soon the message of a crucified, risen and soon coming Saviour might be carried to the whole world" *Messages to Young People*, p. 196.

Let's consider the phrase "rightly trained."

As a church, we look with justifiable pride and joy at our many student missionaries, our outreach and witnessing classes, our student literature evangelists, our Maranatha trips, our seminar teams. Our youth are accomplishing so much good!

But are we really training them seven days a week, 24 hours a day to receive the special outpouring of the Holy Spirit in the Latter Rain? Have we really reached the ideal that God has outlined for His children—an ideal that, if followed, guarantees success?

I've taught at five schools and visited scores of others, and I believe that much of the entertainment we present, or allow our youth to present, makes the angels weep. We do lip service to the principles of purity,[1] sobriety,[2] evangelism,[3] stewardship,[4] modesty,[5] reverence,[6] service,[7] and equality[8] five and a half days a week, and then we undermine it all on Saturday night! If anyone protests, they risk being met with "Loosen up—it's the nineties!"

God hasn't "loosened up" however. His principles remain the same yesterday, today, and forever.[9] His ideals are found in a Book that receives precious little attention, especially as the source of criteria for evaluating Saturday-night entertainment.

Instead of biblical principles guiding our choices, today a lot of our ideas concerning humor and family structure are shaped by the media—especially "Saturday Night Live," but also by a whole

---

1. Matthew 5:8
2. Titus 2:12
3. Matthew 28:19-29
4. Matthew 25:24-28
5. 1 Timothy 2:9
6. Psalm 111:9
7. Isaiah 5:8
8. Galatians 3:28
9. Hebrews 13:8

gamut of other comedy, variety, and talk shows. Nothing is too sacred to these professional laugh makers. What often elicits the greatest laughter is anything related to the magic word *sex*—be it references to adultery, fornication, deviant family structures, or the current in-vogue subject: the war between the sexes.

I submit to you that *none* of the above-mentioned topics are laughing matters—either to God or to the victims of unbiblical sex, be they men or women. Biblical sex is a beautiful, awesome expression of real love and caring, participated in by two persons who are soul mates for life. Adultery and fornication cause bitterness and regret—for a lifetime. Those shattered families are not laughing. And the victims of cruel chauvinism or selfish feminism are not laughing. What is funny about a woman who expected to find companionship and joy in a relationship and instead finds belittling remarks and demeaning behavior? What is funny about a man who longed for tender words, comfort and friendship and instead finds nagging, insults, and rancor?

The relationship between God and His people is symbolized in Scripture by the beauty and completeness of the relationship between a man and a woman. Should we trivialize, cheapen, and degrade something created by God Himself? Yet many of our school-approved videos, movies, skits, and program emcee jokes do just that.

And what about our ethnic jokes, dumb-blonde jokes, and religious traditionalist jokes? Sometimes people don't realize that a particular thing might be offensive to a certain part of society, if they are not part of that segment. Even if a person of a particular gender, race, or religion states, "I don't mind being insulted and slandered," we need to be cognizant of the feelings of those who *do* mind!

Last year I was asked to OK a particular movie for a banquet because the program committee couldn't be called together in time. I liked the movie personally—its style of humor appealed to me, with its play on words and satirical romance. After it was shown, one of my best friends said heatedly, "Cindy, how *could* you approve that movie, with all its violence and references to the occult?"

I was initially irate, *because I liked the movie* and thought it was all in good clean fun—no sex or profanity! But as I thought about the principles he was standing for, I had to admit he was right. A true friend, like a true prophet, will challenge our thinking!

If God raised up Jeremiah, Ezekiel, or Elijah, what would they say about Adventist recreation, including our TV, video, and movie choices? If Martin Luther were a Seventh-day Adventist today, what would be the messages of his 95 theses? And on whose door would he nail them?

According to Jesus' words in Luke 16, it wouldn't do much good to raise up Jeremiah, when the words of Isaiah go unheeded: "He who stops his ears from hearing about bloodshed, and shuts his eyes from looking upon evil; He will dwell on the heights, his refuge will be the impregnable rock; his bread will be given him, his water shall be sure" Isaiah 33: 15,16, NASB.

In other words, if we're really serious about this idea of being part of the Latter Rain and then living victoriously through the time of trouble, we had better make some pretty drastic lifestyle changes. We must be able emphatically to say with David, "I will set no evil thing before my eyes" Psalm 101:3. Our compassionate Saviour eagerly wants to help us carry out that resolve.

And what about our insatiable preoccupation with sports? Jesus says, "No man can serve two masters." Either we're pursuing heaven with every facet of our being, or we're enamored with the things of this world. As adults, what are we saying to our youth about priorities when we can watch a game for hours and study our Bible for minutes? When we know all the essential sporting stats, but can't find the texts that would lead a person to accept Christ as their personal Saviour? When we clap, scream, and shout at a "good play," yet get really nervous when someone gets excited and enthusiastic about the cross of Christ?

"Those who minister to others will . . . not be longing for exciting amusements" *The Desire of Ages*, p. 641.

And yes, I have found through bitter experience that what I eat affects my spirituality, my discernment, and my ability to work effectively for Jesus. Overeating, eating between meals, high intake of sugar and fat, caffeine, and lack of exercise are destructive to this body for which Jesus bled and died. It's not legalism—it's common sense! The less I justify and rationalize and the more of my life I commit to my Saviour, the more freedom I have to enjoy His friendship. And the more energy I have to share the Good News!

Sometimes in life, the easiest thing to do is just to play ostrich—you know, ignore the things that are reprehensible and hope someone else will speak up. After all, everyone likes to have some friends! But then, I am reminded of Ghandi's statement:

"Anything you do will be insignificant, but it is very important that you do it." One thing I hope to teach my witnessing students is the importance of standing for their convictions, even though those convictions may be unpopular.

Our kids are not just willing, but eager to work for God in so many different avenues. All week we try to call people out of the world—why call them back into it on Saturday night?

May all of us be more sensitive to the words of the song, "Lord, let me lift up those who are weak" and determine to make our churches and schools truly loving, Christ-centered families—even at the Talent Show! Then our youth can lighten the earth with God's glory: "Fair as the moon, clear as the sun, and terrible as an army with banners."—1 Song of Solomon 6:10

Witnessing and Outreach

GLAA Witnessing Class meets on Tuesdays for a half hour of instruction.

Mrs. Shirley Gammon, one of the drivers, attends a Witnessing class.

Kathy Blair and Karen Streelman teach a Daniel prophecy lesson in a home.

Robin Hansen and Dan Bowman role play how to begin a Bible study.

Pam Gombrowski and Leslie Nelson assist one of their students with a lesson.

Witnessing class students Holly Dunnebeck and Chris Randall conduct a church service.

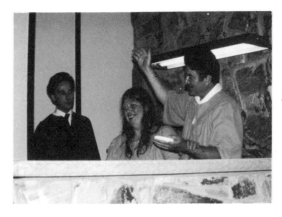

Visiting pastor Jerry LaFave looks on as Pastor Fred Earles prepares to baptize Witnessing Bible student Sharon Miller.

The baptisms on Witnessing Sabbath always bring smiles!

Newly baptized members with Witnessing students and drivers.

Witnessing students sit with their "studies" at potlucks.

The Outreach class prepares a Senior-Citizen Banquet.

Outreach class students make posters for a Neighborhood Story Hour.

EPILOGUE:

Is a teen witness program worth the time and effort? Let a mother who buried her own teen daughter answer this question.

"When Shirley was attending GLAA for grade 11, we encouraged her to participate in the witnessing program. She was rather reluctant and apprehensive about it, and as we parted, she was noncommittal. However, at registration, with Mrs. Tutsch's 'persuasion,' she and a friend signed up.

"To begin with, she was a little fearful and wondered whether she could afford the time required to go to the studies and to prepare for them each week. She also wondered if she wanted to miss out on the recreation at the academy one night every week. As the studies progressed and the lady she was studying with accepted each new truth as it was presented,

Shirley's desire to continue the Bible studies grew. She was so happy when the lady—her first Bible study—accepted Jesus fully, was baptized, and joined the local SDA church.

"Her second year, Shirley had no doubts: she wanted to be part of the witnessing team. When her study that year decided that following Jesus was asking her to give up too much and discontinued the studies, Shirley was anxious to begin another study, even though it was getting near the end of the school year. She encouraged me to attend lay Bible ministries seminars and give Bible studies myself.

"As her senior year at the academy was coming to a close and she was making plans to attend Andrews University, two of her concerns were whether she would be able to continue giving Bible studies there, and how she could help with finances. Opportunities and hopes for employment just did not seem to work out. Then plans for the Detroit Youth Challenge program were made, and Mrs. Tutsch talked to Shirley about participating. She was excited at the prospect and called home immediately, feeling sure that God had answered her prayers.

"As any parent can understand, I was a little apprehensive about my 18-year-old daughter going door to door in this day and age. Another problem was that in the initial planning stages, any student who participated in the program would have to provide his/her own transportation. We had no vehicle available for her to use. Her father and I discussed it and finally decided that—although financially for us it would be a step in the wrong direction and would cost us much more than she would make—other values were more important. We felt that working for the Lord in such a direct way would benefit her more than the financial gain of a different job and prayed that God would protect her and help us provide financially for her education.

"During the summer we appreciated her joy in working for the Lord; her self-reliance and dependability—since she was responsible for seeing that the local group went out faithfully and put in their hours of visiting homes—and her faithful preparation for the Revelation Bible Seminar they were helping to conduct. We knew even then that we had made the right decision.

"Later in the fall, when her father became ill and was diagnosed with pancreatic cancer, she made the statement on several occasions that without the closer walk and dependence on God she had developed during the summer while working with the Detroit Youth Challenge, she wouldn't have been able to cope with her father's illness and death.

"We do not know or understand God's leading in our lives. The witnessing class gave her a better understanding of her own beliefs and a taste of the joy of working for the Lord. The summer with the group built on this. It taught her dependence on God and showed her the necessity of the Holy Spirit's leading in all things. Her father's illness reinforced this dependence on God and showed her the futility of earthly things. It made her realize that the only really important thing was a relationship with Jesus. However, through all of this she did not lose her joy and exuberance in life on this earth.

It just had a new focus—Jesus, and being ready to meet Him. When she died in an auto accident on February 24, 1992, her top priority was to be ready to meet both of her Fathers in heaven."

—*Luvamay Dovich* (Shirley's mother)

Shirley's last Bible study family were baptized together three months after her death.

Shirley Dovich

One Last Appeal

The following letters were given to me spontaneously by people interested in seeing more armies of youth, armed with the Sword of the Spirit—which is the Word of God—advancing into the enemy's territory. I have not edited these letters, except to change the names of those to whom they were addressed.

"Dear faculty, students, and staff of every Adventist school:

"We are two seniors from Great Lakes Adventist Academy. We would like to share with you the ways Witnessing Class has affected our lives and our campus. We have written this letter on our own accord.

"We cannot imagine our lives, at this point, without witnessing. Going to church is no longer a requirement; it's a privilege. Being in Witnessing Class has opened our eyes to our mission in the church and has intensified our relationship with God.

"One aspect of witnessing is the enthusiasm it creates, not only on campus, but within the entire community. Through witnessing, the desire to share the Good News with others is definitely exemplified. The students in our Witnessing Class are much more willing to get involved in religious activities such as: singing bands, sermonettes, public prayers, special music, sharing personal testimonies, vesper programs, Sabbath School, afterglow programs, dormitory prayer groups, and voluntary services in the community.

"Even though a few of these activities were present before Witnessing Class was introduced on our campus, we feel it has had an extremely positive impact on them.

"We have developed some wonderful relationships with the individuals we have given Bible studies to. Seeing these people grow and mature spiritually has, in turn, helped us in the same way. To have a Bible study decide to be baptized is one of the most thrilling experiences that can happen in a person's life. The feeling is . . . beyond words! We have developed with them a friendship that will last throughout eternity.

"We personally feel that without Witnessing Class, we would not have the firm foundation that presently ties us to the church and draws us closer to God. In the future, we fully intend to continue with and expand upon the philosophy we have learned while in this class. We want to be an integral part of our church in the future and hope to hasten Christ's coming.

"We implore you to consider all the ramifications that a witnessing program could have on your campus. Witnessing has virtually become a way of life, not only for ourselves, but for our classmates as well.

"'Then said I: "Ah, Lord God! Behold, I cannot speak, for I am a youth." But the Lord said to me: "Do not say, 'I am a youth,' For you shall go to all to whom I send you, and whatever I command you, you shall speak."' Jeremiah 1:6, 7.

"We will be praying for you.

"Your friends in Christ, Daniel Knapp [Senior Class President] and Robin Hansen."

"To the Michigan Conference Administration:

"Kay and I want to express our sincere appreciation for the privilege of working with Cindy and her youthful leaders in the Carson City church, and for the wonderful opportunity to become better acquainted with them personally.

"It has been such a heart-warming experience to see her determination to see our youth excel, not just in the scholastic attainments, but in their own personal relationship with Jesus and in heart to heart, door to door, actual spiritual contact with hungering souls.

"It is so inspiring to see young people catch the vision that they can serve God effectively, even now, while they are receiving a Christian education. The highest quality of education it is possible to give our youth is to encourage them to become actively engaged in giving Bible studies, learning how to conduct Revelation Seminars, preaching sermons, teaching Sabbath School classes, and actually learning how to operate a church by becoming personally involved in all its functions—from sitting on the church board to paying the bills, serving as leaders, and reaching into the community to make a difference in the lives of those to whom they minister.

"I earnestly pray that every school administrator, every teacher, and every member of the faculty and staff of all our elementary schools, academies, and colleges can catch the vision of what God has inspired Cindy—and those who support her witnessing and outreach ministry at Great Lakes Adventist Academy—to accomplish in training our youth.

"May the vision spread like wildfire throughout the entire world field. God started the work of the Seventh-day Adventist Church with young people, and He will bring it to its final, glorious triumph through the lives and witness of dedicated, loving, and loveable Christian youth.

"Sincerely your friend throughout eternity, Dan G. Collins" [Michigan Conference Evangelist]

I can only say again, *"Not to us, O Lord, not to us, but to thy name give glory, because of thy lovingkindness, because of thy truth." Psalm 115:1,* NASB.

APPENDIX

PERSONAL TESTIMONY WORKSHEET

"How I Discovered Life At Its Best"

MY LIFE BEFORE I ACCEPTED CHRIST:

What was it like? (Lonely, insecure, guilt-ridden, aimless)

"I needed help."—8T 321

HOW I FOUND CHRIST:

Tell how it happened (evangelistic meetings, Bible studies, friend, tragedy, etc.)

"I found the Bible the voice of God to my soul."—8T 321

MY LIFE SINCE I FOUND CHRIST:

Tell of the change, the joys, the blessings. (I found peace, hope for the future, security knowing that God controls my life and the world, etc.)

"In Christ the hunger of my soul has been satisfied."—8T321

Use an appropriate Scripture which sums up your testimony, to climax.

COMMUNITY RELIGIOUS SURVEY

A. Concerning God and the Bible:
  1. In your opinion, is there a God?
    ❏ Yes   ❏ No   ❏ No opinion
  2. Is there life after death?
    ❏ Yes   ❏ No   ❏ No opinion
  3. Is Christ coming again?
    ❏ Yes   ❏ No   ❏ No opinion
  4. Who is Jesus, according to your understanding?
    ❏ Son of God
    ❏ Savior of man
    ❏ Prophet
    ❏ Creator
    ❏ Not sure
  5. Do you feel you understand the Bible?
    ❏ Yes   ❏ No   ❏ No opinion

B. Concerning religious involvement:
  6. What Church did your parents attend?
    _____
  7. Do you belong to the same church?_____
  8. How often do you attend?
    ❏ Weekly
    ❏ Monthly
    ❏ Seldom
    ❏ Never
  9. Do you believe all churches should unite?
    ❏ Yes   ❏ No   ❏ No opinion

C. Your opinion:
  10. Why do you think so many youth today are turning to spiritual things?

  11. How does one become a Christian?

FREE BIBLE!

Participate in the Bible reading guide plan and receive your own personal King James version hard-cover Bible.

Become better acquainted with your Bible and your God. Clip the coupon and mail today!

Yes! I desire to participate in the Bible Reading Plan. I understand that there is no financial obligation.

Name_____

Street address_____

City_____Zip_____

Mail to GLAA/CT, Box 19009, Lansing, MI